Original title:
Lost in Love

Copyright © 2024 Swan Charm
All rights reserved.

Author: Mirell Mesipuu
ISBN HARDBACK: 978-9916-79-197-4
ISBN PAPERBACK: 978-9916-79-198-1
ISBN EBOOK: 978-9916-79-199-8

Pilgrimage of the Heart

In shadows deep, the heart does roam,
Seeking whispers of His holy home.
Each step adorned with faith anew,
In the quiet night, His love breaks through.

Through valleys low and mountains high,
I walk with grace under the sky.
Every tear, a prayer I sow,
Trusting His light to guide me so.

With every breath, a sacred vow,
In His presence, I humbly bow.
The journey unfolds, the path divine,
In the pilgrimage of the heart, I shine.

Among the stars, His voice does sing,
Reminding me of the joys He brings.
In moments lost, I find my place,
In the arms of love, a warm embrace.

The Relics of Our Togetherness

In the tapestry of life we weave,
Each thread a bond, we believe.
In shared embraces, warmth ignites,
The relics of love in shining lights.

Through trials faced and joys embraced,
In the heart's chamber, memories traced.
A song of faith, our spirits sing,
Together, we rise, in Him we cling.

In laughter shared, in silence held,
The sacred moments, forever spelled.
Everlasting in His design,
A promise made, our souls entwine.

Among the echoes, our voices blend,
In His grace, our stories mend.
With each dawn, our hearts will find,
The relics of love, through His grace defined.

Ruins of a Love Once Adored

In starlit nights, our love was born,
In innocence, we were once adorned.
A fire burned within our souls,
But shadows came and stole our goals.

In whispered dreams, we used to soar,
Yet time eroded what we adored.
Now in ruins, the heart stands bare,
An echo of love, a solemn prayer.

We traced the paths where laughter danced,
In faded light, we took our chance.
Yet the walls of memory now confine,
What once was holy, now is divine.

Yet hope lingers in silent cries,
For love reborn through tear-filled eyes.
In ruins lies a seed of grace,
With every loss, we find our place.

The Lord's Lament for Us

Upon the earth, His spirit weeps,
In humble moments, His promise keeps.
With outstretched hands, He calls our name,
In the silence, He bears our shame.

In trials faced and burdens borne,
The Lord stands by, His heart worn.
In every struggle, every plight,
He walks beside us, our guiding light.

In the depths of night, He softly cries,
For the lost souls who seek the skies.
He gathers tears, a soothing balm,
In the chaos, His presence calm.

Oh, seek His love in fragile space,
In every heart, He leaves His trace.
His lament echoes, a call so true,
Forever longing, He waits for you.

When Saints Weep for Love's Fragment

In quiet chambers, whispers soar,
Hearts laid bare, shadows implore.
Between the silence, sorrow flows,
For love's pure light, the darkness knows.

Saints, with tear-streaked faces dim,
Seek the fragments lost in hymn.
Their voices blend, a soft lament,
For every moment, love was spent.

Radiant souls, they wander wide,
Holding tight to hope inside.
With every heartbeat, echoes plead,
For love's embrace, their spirits bleed.

Through peeling layers of despair,
They cast their gaze in fervent prayer.
In fleeting glances, warmth ignites,
Uniting souls on starry nights.

When hearts collide in sacred space,
Awake the ache, a holy grace.
For love, though lost, ignites the flame,
In every saint, the eternal name.

Ascetic Yearning in a Fleeting Realm

In cloistered realms where shadows creep,
The heart awakes, no longer sleep.
Forsaking joys of earthly ride,
In sacred stillness, whispers guide.

Fragrant incense fills the air,
Each breath a prayer, a soul laid bare.
In hunger's grip, they find their way,
Each silent vow, their spirits sway.

With every fast, they seek the light,
In starry veils, through darkest night.
A yearning deep, to touch the divine,
In fleeting realms, their hearts entwine.

The world outside, a distant call,
Within these walls, they rise and fall.
In ascetic bliss, they dance apart,
In every silence, speaks the heart.

So lift your gaze to skies above,
In tranquil realms, embrace the love.
For in detachment, life reveals,
The sacred truths that feeling steals.

Whispers of the Divine Heart

In stillness, prayer lifts to the skies,
A soft light bathes where the spirit lies.
Echoes of love in the sacred night,
Hearts entwined in a glorious sight.

The gentle breeze carries sweet refrain,
Whispers of hope where there is no pain.
A promise etched in the stars above,
Each heartbeat sings of everlasting love.

In twilight's glow, faith begins to rise,
The soul finds solace, in Truth it flies.
With every shadow, the light draws near,
In the hush of dawn, the end of fear.

The heart knows paths where angels tread,
Guided by grace, though waters spread.
In silence, wisdom unveils the light,
Whispers of peace in the morning bright.

So let the heart ache with longing's call,
For in surrender, we rise or fall.
Abide in love, let your spirit soar,
Whispers of the Divine evermore.

Pilgrimage of the Wandering Soul

On ancient roads, the spirit roams,
Seeking shelter far from earthly homes.
With each step, the heart learns to bend,
The journey's path begins to mend.

In valleys deep, where shadows loom,
The new dawn's light shatters the gloom.
Through deserts dry, and oceans wide,
Faith as a compass, a constant guide.

The mountain's peak calls the weary hearts,
Where each new beginning, the spirit imparts.
In every prayer, the soul finds its voice,
A dance of hope in the sacred choice.

O, wandering soul, embrace the hill,
With faith ignited, the heart to fill.
Though storms may rise and shadows cast,
Your pilgrimage leads to blessings vast.

So tread with courage, the sacred ground,
In whispers of grace, your truths profound.
With every step, draw closer to grace,
In the pilgrimage, find your place.

Sacred Echoes of a Faded Embrace

In the silence of night, memories bloom,
The essence of love dispels the gloom.
Echoes of laughter in every sigh,
Faded yet vibrant, spirits fly high.

With each heartbeat, the past does call,
A gentle reminder, the greatest gift of all.
Though faces may fade, the love remains,
In sacred whispers, the heart attains.

Through veils of time, with gentle care,
The threads of the heart weave memories rare.
In every embrace that once was close,
The soul finds solace, and love engross.

So gather the fragments, let them collide,
In the sacred echoes, let love abide.
For even in fading, love's light prevails,
In the tapestry woven, unity sails.

With gratitude's grace, cherish the light,
In the echoes of love, the heart takes flight.
Though the embrace may fade, the spirit knows,
In sacred whispers, true love forever flows.

The Sanctuary of Unspoken Longings

In secret chambers, the heart concealed,
Whispers of yearning, yet unrevealed.
Soft shadows dance where hope takes flight,
In the sanctuary of the velvet night.

Each thought a prayer, each sigh a plea,
In silence deep, the soul longs to be free.
Amidst the echoes of dreams unmet,
The heart seeks a path that won't forget.

With every dawn, new light will break,
Illuminating desires that softly ache.
In the hush of morning, truth shall rise,
Each unspoken wish, under vast skies.

So linger in moments, let love unfold,
Within sacred spaces, the truth grows bold.
For in the silence, connections ignite,
In the sanctuary, hearts burn bright.

Embrace the longing, let passion steer,
For in the depths, divinity is near.
Through unspoken dreams, the spirit finds,
The sanctuary of love that ever binds.

Divine Dust on Forgotten Altars

In shadows long, where silence weeps,
The dust of prayers, in shadows keeps.
Lost whispers rise, like incense sweet,
On altars bare, where spirits meet.

Forgotten hymns, in echoes blend,
Each note a plea, each sigh a friend.
The light of hope, a flicker shines,
In sacred space, where love entwines.

O humble heart, your gifts laid down,
In quiet grace, a velvet gown.
With every tear, a memory finds,
The strength of faith in gentle binds.

Through ancient stones, a story flows,
Of grace divine, where mercy grows.
Each crack a testament of time,
In brokenness, we are made prime.

So gather close, in twilight's glow,
Embrace the dusk, where spirits flow.
For in the dust, life's whispers dwell,
In forgotten altars, peace shall swell.

The Grace of Moments Unheld

In fleeting time, where shadows play,
We chase the light, we yearn, we pray.
Each heartbeat sings a silent song,
Of moments lost, yet ever strong.

In gentle winds, the spirit calls,
Through open skies, where love enthralls.
Each glance a gift, unwrapped with care,
A dance of souls, in sacred air.

The grace of now, a tender touch,
In simple acts, we find so much.
With hands entwined, the world we face,
In every breath, we find our grace.

Through joy and pain, through hope and fear,
In moments brief, the truth is clear.
For time is but a fleeting friend,
In each embrace, our hearts transcend.

So hold the light, within your chest,
In love's embrace, we find our rest.
For every moment, though unheld,
In divine grace, our souls are swelled.

Songs of Desolation in Sacred Silence

In barren lands, where shadows creep,
The songs of sorrow, softly weep.
Through aching voids, the spirit cries,
In sacred silence, where hope dies.

In every stone, a prayer resides,
A yearning heart, where faith abides.
Each note of grief, a whisper's thread,
In desolation, the soul is fed.

Yet from the depths, a voice will rise,
Transforming pain to purest skies.
In twilight's hush, the echoes bloom,
A symphony that breaks the gloom.

With every tear, a flower grows,
In barren soil, a truth bestows.
The songs of desolation weave,
A tapestry of hearts that believe.

So listen close, to silence loud,
In shadows cast, we stand unbowed.
For in the void, sweet grace is found,
In sacred silence, love's profound.

Reflections on a Twilight Prayer

As twilight dims, the stars awake,
We raise our hearts, for love's own sake.
In whispered thoughts, a prayer released,
In twilight's glow, our souls find peace.

The dusk caresses, a gentle guide,
Where faith and doubt, together bide.
With every breath, the universe sings,
In quiet corners, the spirit clings.

In softening light, our hearts align,
Each moment shared, a sacred sign.
With humble words, the heavens bend,
In twilight prayer, where spirits mend.

The night will come, but still we glow,
For love endures, through ebb and flow.
In reflections bright, a promise clear,
Our twilight prayer will persevere.

So gather close, as shadows blend,
In silent vows, our hearts transcend.
For in the dusk, we find our way,
In twilight prayers, we choose to stay.

The Temple of Echoes Yet Unheard

In shadows deep where silence dwells,
A whispered prayer, a heart that swells.
Voices lost in sacred space,
Yearning souls, we seek His grace.

Beneath the arch of twilight skies,
Hope lingers soft, our spirit flies.
Each echo borne on golden light,
Guides us through the endless night.

With every step, the echoes call,
In unity, we shall not fall.
From stone to flesh, we find our way,
A dance of love in bright array.

In this temple, the heartbeats blend,
Our voices rise, the wounds we mend.
Yet unheard, a hymn of peace,
In sacred trust, our fears release.

Ascension Through the Veil of Grief

Beneath the weight of sorrow's shroud,
We search for light, we cry aloud.
In tears, we find the strength to rise,
Transcending pain, embracing skies.

Each mourning star a guide above,
A beacon of unfailing love.
Through shadows thick, we walk the line,
In grief's embrace, our hearts entwine.

The veil is thin, the spirits soar,
In whispered hopes, we seek for more.
With every breath, a prayer ascends,
Uniting souls, where sorrow ends.

From ashes, faith begins to glow,
As seeds of joy begin to grow.
In every loss, the light we find,
Ascension born of love entwined.

Chronicles of the Heart's Pilgrimage

A journey starts where faith resides,
Across the plains, where hope abides.
In every step, a story penned,
A testament to love's extend.

Through valleys low, we learn to trust,
In trials faced, we find the just.
With open hearts, we heed the call,
In unity, together, fall.

The lessons learned in gentle grace,
As time unveils the sacred space.
Each winding path, a guide to see,
The truth of love, our tapestry.

With every compass, hearts align,
In sacred whispers, the spirit shines.
Each chronicle, a page of light,
In faith's embrace, we find our flight.

The Unfinished Prayer of Togetherness

In harmony, our voices blend,
A prayer unspoken, hearts extend.
Together found, in silence shared,
An unfinished song, the soul laid bare.

Threads of love in every tear,
Binding us close, dispelling fear.
In each embrace, the promise lives,
A sacred bond, the spirit gives.

Yet in the stillness, hope unfolds,
A call to all, the meek and bold.
Through every hardship, we shall stand,
An unfinished prayer, hand in hand.

For love's alignment knows no end,
An endless journey, we transcend.
Together we rise, unbroken and free,
In the unfinished prayer, our unity.

The Sacred Rites of Heartache

In the silence, whispers dwell,
Echoes of love, a sorrowed bell.
Vows once spoken, now drift away,
In aching hearts, we silently pray.

Yearning for comfort, a gentle hand,
Lost in the shadows, we barely stand.
Hope flickers dim in the soul's deep night,
Guided by faith, we seek the light.

The temple of memories, holy ground,
Where every tear falls, grace is found.
In anguish, the spirit learns to rise,
To mend the fractures, to touch the skies.

With every heartbeat, a lesson learned,
From the ashes of love, a fire burned.
We gather the pieces, though weary and torn,
In the rituals of grief, new life is born.

The sacred rites of heartache unfold,
In the depth of despair, our stories are told.
Together we wander, no longer alone,
In suffering's cradle, our souls have grown.

The Pilgrim's Lament

Upon the path, a pilgrim strides,
With heavy heart where sorrow abides.
Each step echoes with longing's plea,
Searching for solace, for comfort to see.

Beneath the sky, vast and unkind,
Winds carry whispers of love left behind.
Eyes turned upwards in desperate prayer,
Longing for guidance, a way to repair.

Streets of stone lead to the door,
Where memories linger, a haunting lore.
In shadows tossed, secrets entwine,
The heart's true home, lost in time.

Through every trial, a lesson sown,
In lonely nights, our faith has grown.
With open hands, we gather the tears,
Turning heartache into sacred years.

The pilgrim journeys, a quest divine,
In every lament, our souls realign.
With every heartbeat, a prayer takes flight,
In the midst of sorrow, we seek the light.

Rituals of the Lost Lover

In the twilight, shadows blend,
Where echoes of love seem to transcend.
Whispers linger in the moonlight's glow,
In the heart's deep ache, a love we know.

Each memory woven in sacred thread,
A tapestry of tears that we have shed.
In silent rituals, we call your name,
In the ashes of longing, we fan the flame.

With every glance at the empty chair,
In the breath of night, you linger there.
A soul entwined, yet worlds apart,
In the silence, you dwell in my heart.

Time passes slowly in this endless dance,
Weaving the past in a fleeting glance.
As the dawn breaks, we hold our breath,
In rituals sacred, we embrace the depth.

The lost lover's song, a haunting refrain,
In the heart of the night, a sacred pain.
Through every heartbeat, love's echo flows,
In the rituals of loss, our spirit knows.

The Veil Between Us

A veil hangs lightly on the breeze,
Between our souls, a yearning tease.
In the stillness, a sacred space,
Where heartbeats echo, love's embrace.

Through the fabric of time, we reach,
In silence's language, the heart can teach.
Though distance stretches, we stand as one,
In shadows dancing, our spirits run.

The stars bear witness, our love divine,
In the heavens, our fates align.
Yet here on earth, the chords remain,
Bound by the love, entwined in pain.

Every sigh is a prayer at night,
In the depths of longing, we find the light.
With every breath, the veil grows thin,
Our souls intertwine, where love begins.

In the sacred depths, we find our way,
Through the veil between us, night and day.
Though apart, our hearts forever share,
The bond of love, a timeless prayer.

The Lost Rosary of Kindred Spirits

In the hush of the twilight's embrace,
Rests a rosary, tethered by grace.
Each bead a whisper, a prayer once sung,
Binding souls together, forever young.

Through shadows of longing, we search in vain,
For the echoes of laughter, the joy, the pain.
With every heartbeat, the spirits align,
In the tapestry woven, our hearts intertwine.

Beneath the stars' gaze, they gather near,
Rekindling the hope drowned in deep-seated fear.
The lost rosary glimmers, a beacon bright,
In the depths of our sorrow, it guides us to light.

In silence we build, on the strength of the past,
Uniting in faith, a bond that will last.
A reminder of kindness, of love's gentle grace,
In the lost rosary, we find our place.

Beneath the Weeping Ash Tree

Beneath the ash tree, ancient and wise,
Whispers of solace fill the skies.
Each drooping branch tells tales of old,
Of hearts once weary, and spirits bold.

In its shadow we gather, hands intertwined,
Seeking the warmth of the love we find.
The petals of hope fall soft to the ground,
In this sacred haven, our peace is found.

Through seasons that change and storms that arrive,
The ash stands steadfast, helping us thrive.
We share our secrets, our prayers in the breeze,
As the world spins on, we find our ease.

Underneath its boughs, we quietly dream,
Of unity born from the softest gleam.
With every raindrop, with every sigh,
We rise like the sun, together we try.

Parables of the Heart's Absence

In the silence between each breath we take,
Lies the parable of hearts that ache.
The absence of love, a shadowed refrain,
Whispered in moments of yearning and pain.

Each lonely echo a story to tell,
Of bonds left broken, and wishes that fell.
In the void of connection, we search for light,
Finding solace in the stars of the night.

Through lessons of patience, in hearts made anew,
We learn from the absence what love can pursue.
The parables guide us, gentle and true,
In the tapestry woven of old and of new.

Each tear that has fallen, a seed of regret,
In the garden of longing, our spirits beget.
From absence to presence, we forge our way,
In the warmth of the love that will never betray.

Treading on Holy Ground of Remembrance

On holy ground, where memories bloom,
We tread with respect, dispelling the gloom.
Echoes of laughter, the kiss of the past,
In the chambers of time, our shadows are cast.

Amidst whispered prayers, the stillness we share,
Brings comfort and grace, a balm for our care.
In the sacred embrace of all we hold dear,
We honor their journeys, the paths they endear.

With every footstep, we gather the light,
Rekindling spirits that take to their flight.
Through the veils of remembrance, we walk hand in hand,

A circle of love, where we forever stand.

Treading on ground where the sacred once lay,
In the depths of our hearts, we find a way.
To celebrate life and all that it brings,
In the realm of remembrance, our spirit sings.

The Wounded Disciple of Desire

In shadows cast by yearning's cries,
The heart beats strong, yet weighed with sighs.
A soul in torment, yet grasping grace,
In every wound, a sacred place.

The ember glows in darkened night,
A flicker frail, yet burning bright.
Desire's chains, they bind and tear,
Yet in this pain, love's whispers share.

With every step on earth so cold,
The stories of redemption told.
A journey marked by trials endured,
In every wound, the faith assured.

So let the tears of anguish fall,
Like prayers that rise; they heed the call.
For in despair, the spirit wakes,
And through the heart, the Savior breaks.

An Epistle to the Dearest Departed

Oh, gentle soul, who walks above,
A silent song of endless love.
Your echoes dance on evening's breath,
In whispered hopes beyond all death.

With every star that fills the night,
I feel your warmth, that tender light.
Though time may wear this weary frame,
Your essence lingers, sweet and tame.

In sacred texts, your name I write,
Each letter kissed by twilight's light.
A bond unbroken, strong and true,
In silent prayers, I'll remember you.

As seasons change and shadows wane,
Your love remains, a soft refrain.
To you, dear heart, my words I send,
In faith's embrace, we shall ascend.

The Benediction of Hallowed Longing

In yearning hearts, a blessing lies,
A sacred song that never dies.
With open hands, we seek the skies,
And in our faith, true love defies.

Each breath a prayer, each heartbeat sings,
To God above, in faith, we cling.
In passions pure, our spirits soar,
Anointed hearts forevermore.

The longing deep, a sacred fire,
Ignites the soul with pure desire.
Through trials faced and tears we weep,
In hallowed longing, love runs deep.

So let us hold the dream sublime,
In every dusk, in every clime.
For in the depths, true joy we find,
A benediction intertwined.

Hymns of the Unseen

In realms beyond what eyes can see,
A harmony flows endlessly.
With every note, the spirits rise,
In choir's grace, they pierce the skies.

The unseen light, our guiding star,
In whispered hymns, we travel far.
Through valleys deep and mountains high,
In sacred echoes, we defy.

The heartbeats sing a timeless tune,
Beneath the sun, beneath the moon.
Each silent prayer a sacred thread,
In unity, our spirits led.

With outstretched arms, we seek the dawn,
To lift the veil, our fears are gone.
In every sigh, the hush of peace,
In hymns of love, may sorrows cease.

Fragments of Joy

In morning light, the spirit sings,
With whispered prayer, the heart takes wing.
In every breath, a sacred spark,
Guiding souls through the endless dark.

Soft echoes dance on tender grace,
In each small moment, we find our place.
The world unfolds in colors bright,
While shadows fade within the light.

Joy arises from the depths of woe,
In every tear, a chance to grow.
With faith as our unwavering guide,
We walk together, side by side.

In laughter shared, the heart rejoices,
Within the stillness, we hear the voices.
Fragments of joy, like stars at night,
Illuminate paths, all wrongs made right.

Shattered Whispers

In broken whispers, prayers ascend,
Each sorrow and joy, they blend.
In silent nights, the heart does weep,
Yet through the cracks, love's promise seeps.

Amidst despair, a faint light glows,
Shattered dreams, their beauty shows.
With every wound, a lesson learned,
In fragile moments, our spirits yearn.

Voices call from the distant past,
In echoes of grace, we find what's cast.
The threads of hope entwined with pain,
In shattered whispers, love sustains.

In the stillness, a promise lies,
For each goodbye, a new sunrise.
Shattered whispers make us whole,
In brokenness, we find our soul.

In the Shadow of the Divine

In shadows deep, the spirits dwell,
Whispering secrets, a timeless spell.
With open hearts, we seek the light,
In the shadow of the Divine so bright.

The mountains stand as guardians tall,
In silence, we hear the sacred call.
The stars above, a pathway drawn,
Guiding the lost toward the dawn.

In every breath, a chance to heal,
In grace bestowed, our wounds conceal.
In the shadow, love's embrace,
A holy refuge, a cherished space.

Through trials faced and journeys long,
In the shadow, our spirits throng.
With open arms, we intertwine,
In the depths of faith, we find the sign.

Offering the Heart to Eternal Night

In the twilight, we lay our fears,
Offering the heart, with humble tears.
To the eternal night, we release,
In surrender, we find our peace.

The stars bore witness to our plight,
In silence, they yearn for the light.
Through the darkness, our hopes ignite,
An offering made to the vast night.

With each heartbeat, whispers soar,
In surrender, we embrace the core.
Offering our souls, we rise above,
In the night's embrace, we find pure love.

In shadows deep, our spirits twine,
Offering the heart, a sacred sign.
With every evening's gentle flight,
We seek the dawn from eternal night.

The Mysticism of Remembered Kisses

In gentle moments, time stands still,
The mysticism of a lover's thrill.
In whispered dreams, our souls entwine,
With every kiss, a sense divine.

The echoes linger in tender grace,
In memories stitched, we find our place.
Each soft caress, a prayer once heard,
In silent vows, our hearts conferred.

The magic blooms in twilight's glow,
As whispered secrets continue to flow.
In every kiss, the world transforms,
Through shared communion, love conforms.

In the stillness, our spirits find,
The mysticism, beautifully entwined.
In remembered kisses, we ascend,
A sacred journey that knows no end.

Confessions at the Threshold of Heaven

In whispers soft, my heart does plead,
Forgiveness sought, in every deed.
The angels wait, their wings outspread,
As I release my fears and dread.

With trembling steps, I near the gate,
Embraced by love, I shed my weight.
Each secret shared, each sin laid bare,
The light of grace begins to flare.

The path to peace is paved with prayer,
A journey deep, beyond compare.
I find my voice, it starts to rise,
A melody that fills the skies.

With every tear, the soul is healed,
In truth and faith, my heart revealed.
I offer thanks for lessons learned,
For every fire, my spirit burned.

At Heaven's edge, I breathe anew,
A life transformed, my vision true.
In unity, we all can stand,
Together held by His strong hand.

A Psalm for the Forsaken

O Lord, beneath this heavy sky,
Your children weep, and question why.
In shadows cast, their hearts so torn,
In silent nights, they feel forlorn.

Yet in the dark, Your presence glows,
A gentle breath when sorrow flows.
In every cry, a glimmer found,
Your love, O God, knows no bounds.

The lonely walk a narrow road,
With burdens great, they bear their load.
But faith's a light that guides the lost,
Reminding them of love's great cost.

A spirit crushed, yet hope remains,
In darkest hours, love breaks the chains.
For in our pain, Your heart we trace,
You hold the lost in warm embrace.

So let us sing a hymn of grace,
In every heart, let joy find space.
For those who wander, far and wide,
Are welcomed home, with arms spread wide.

The Grace of Unanswered Prayers

In silence, Lord, I seek your face,
In longing hearts, I find my place.
The prayers I cast like seeds on stone,
Yet I am not forsaken, alone.

For every plea that met the sky,
A deeper purpose, I can't deny.
The answers wait, though veiled in night,
A flicker here, a spark of light.

With hands uplifted, I learn to trust,
Your timing, Lord, is ever just.
In waiting still, my heart finds peace,
Each moment lent is love's increase.

In shadows deep, new paths unfold,
To guide my heart to realms of gold.
Though words may falter, grace endures,
In quiet faith, my spirit soars.

Unanswered prayers, like winding roads,
Lead me to where my spirit glows.
For in the stillness, I discern,
The lessons learned, the heart must yearn.

A Angel's Tear in the Sanctum

In sacred halls where angels tread,
A tear descends for souls misled.
With tender grace, it pools below,
A gift of love in softest glow.

The heavy heart that bends in pain,
Find solace here, where hope will reign.
In every drop, a story flows,
Of battles fought, and faith that grows.

A fragile light shines in the gloom,
Like wildflowers that push through bloom.
For in this holy, hallowed space,
Despair gives way to boundless grace.

The angel weeps for hearts that stray,
Yet lifts them high, to brighter day.
With every tear, a promise clear,
In love's embrace, we conquer fear.

So let us gather, hand in hand,
In every tear, a love withstands.
For in the sanctum, spirits rise,
A testament to heaven's ties.

Stars that Only Burned Once

In the quiet night, they gleamed so bright,
A fleeting grace, a sacred light.
Whispers of hope, dreams unspun,
Eternal love, though they've just begun.

In the tapestry of the endless skies,
They dance as spirits, through our sighs.
A memory sweet, etched in time,
Their flickers fade, yet hearts still climb.

For every spark that lights the dark,
Reminds us of life, a sacred mark.
In shadows cast by journeys long,
Their essence lingers, in love's song.

So cherish the brief, the moments rare,
In the hands of fate, we leave our care.
Each star that burns, a tale untold,
In the cosmos vast, our hearts unfold.

The Echo of Two Souls Apart

In silence deep, two spirits wane,
Bound by love, yet marred by pain.
An echo calls, their hearts reach wide,
In the void between, where dreams collide.

Once intertwined, now skies divide,
A symphony, where shadows hide.
Each tear that falls, a prayer in flight,
Longing for dawn, to end the night.

Through valleys low, where sorrows tread,
The winds sing soft of words unsaid.
In every heartbeat, a gentle plea,
For the light of hope, to set them free.

Yet in the dark, their voices blend,
A sacred hymn, that will not end.
Distance may part, but love remains,
In every echo, their heart attains.

Archangels of the Heart

Guardians of love, with wings spread wide,
In shadows cast, they gently guide.
With whispers sweet, and hands of grace,
They mend the wounds, in warm embrace.

In trials faced, they stand beside,
An unseen force, our faithful guide.
When sorrow weighs, and hope is thin,
Their light ignites the flame within.

Through storms they soar, on winds of prayer,
Their essence nurtures, a love laid bare.
In every heart, their blessing flows,
A melody soft, as creation grows.

Embrace the warmth, they freely share,
In every pause, their love is near.
Archangels bright, our souls they lift,
In every moment, a sacred gift.

Surrendered at the Crossroads

At twilight's hour, the paths converge,
Souls in silence, with hearts that urge.
A choice awaits, in the dimming light,
To let go fears, and embrace the fight.

With trembling hands, they seek the truth,
In love's embrace, the spark of youth.
Each step they take, a prayer unspoken,
In faith they walk, though spirits broken.

The world may turn, its shadows cast,
Yet in their souls, a fire holds fast.
With courage found in every breath,
They dance with grace, defying death.

In surrender sweet, they find their way,
Guided by light, into a new day.
At crossroads met, with hearts aglow,
In love's embrace, the truth will flow.

Blessings of a Wounded Heart

In silence I seek, a gentle light,
Whispers of grace in the depth of night.
Crimson tears flow, yet hope remains,
Wounds remind me where true love gains.

Be comforted soul, for pain can teach,
In brokenness, the spirit will reach.
Every scar tells a story divine,
In the shadows, your heart shall shine.

Embrace the warmth of the tender sun,
For healing begins when the battle is won.
Loss is a garden where love can grow,
The blessings of wounds in hearts we sow.

Prayer Beads of Lost Affection

Each bead a moment, a whisper, a prayer,
Threaded with memories, love's sweet snare.
Fingers trace paths where our laughter flowed,
In the fabric of time, our stories are sowed.

Echoes of passion, softly they call,
In the silence that lingers, I hear it all.
Woven in heartstrings, the past holds tight,
Until the dawn breaks the cloak of night.

With every recitation, a tear falls free,
For what was once ours is now memory.
Yet in this lament, there's beauty profound,
In prayer beads of loss, love's essence is found.

Conversations with the Celestial

Beneath the stars, I whisper my dreams,
In the vast expanse, the universe beams.
Angels gather where soft shadows lay,
Their voices lift me, guiding my way.

Questions of fate, I tenderly pose,
In the hush of night, revelation flows.
Each twinkle a script, each comet a sign,
In celestial realms, my spirit aligns.

Listen closely, for wisdom is near,
In moments of stillness, the path becomes clear.
Conversations sacred, eternally soar,
With the divine, I am evermore.

The Ghost of You in Sacred Spaces

In quiet corners, your presence lingers,
Ghostly whispers trace the air with fingers.
In every shadow, your laughter I find,
A haunting beauty, forever entwined.

Candles flicker, casting spells of old,
Tales of our love in the embers bold.
Memories dance in the flickering light,
The ghost of you haunts the edge of night.

Through sacred spaces, I wander alone,
With echoes of love that feel like home.
In a heart once full, now aching and bare,
The ghost of you whispers a timeless prayer.

Beneath the Cloak of Mourning

In shadows deep where silence dwells,
A heart breaks soft, and time compels.
The echoes of a whispered prayer,
Ride waves of grief, ascend the air.

Each tear a gem, in sorrow's grasp,
A soul entwined, in love's sweet clasp.
Beneath the cloak of evening's shroud,
A light still shines, though dimmed, unbowed.

We gather near, in whispered night,
With faith that holds through darkest plight.
Our voices lift, a sacred song,
To honor those who still belong.

The stars above, like candles flame,
Illuminate the heart's refrain.
For in the dark, hope finds a way,
And love endures through night and day.

In mourning's grip, we find our peace,
A balm for hearts that yearn for ease.
We walk together, hand in hand,
Under the gaze of a watchful strand.

An Offering in the Temple of Memory

In the quiet halls where echoes dwell,
We gather dreams, a sacred shell.
An offering laid at memory's feet,
A flame of love, both fierce and sweet.

With every word, a prayer ascends,
For every heart that time transcends.
The altar made of whispered grace,
Reflects the light of each dear face.

In reverence, we bow our heads,
For all the paths our spirit treads.
A fragrant bloom, for those we've lost,
Their laughter lingers, despite the cost.

We clasp our hands, united strong,
Our voices rise, a sacred song.
Memory's temple, forever stands,
Within our hearts, where love commands.

Each moment cherished, never fades,
A tapestry that time pervades.
In this temple, we find the light,
An offering of love so bright.

The Sacrament of What Once Was

In twilight's hush, we find the past,
The sacred moments, forever cast.
With open hearts, we seek the truth,
In every shadow, the glow of youth.

A sacrament of breath and sigh,
We hold the memories, never die.
In silence deep, a prayer takes flight,
For all the days that ended bright.

With every dawn, a chance reborn,
We weave together the grief, the scorn.
The threads of time eternal spin,
A legacy that lies within.

In sacred bond, we find our place,
In shared remembrance, we embrace.
The echoes of the love we knew,
In every heart, they still ring true.

The sacrament of what once was,
A testament, without pause.
In every tear, a story told,
In every hug, a heart of gold.

Temptation in the Garden of Sorrow

In the garden where shadows play,
Whispers haunt the end of day.
Temptation waits with bated breath,
In thorny fields of love and death.

Beneath the boughs, a choice to make,
The fruit of pain, a heart could break.
Yet hope still blooms in tender smiles,
In spite of sorrow's fateful trials.

The serpent's song, a lure so sweet,
With every tear, we feel defeat.
But grace descends, a balm to bear,
In whispered prayers, we find our care.

In every wound, the light can seep,
A promise made, forever keep.
Temptation fades when faith is strong,
In love's embrace, where we belong.

Through darkest nights, a dawn will rise,
To pierce the veil of sorrowed skies.
In every heart, the garden grows,
A testament to love that knows.

Stained Glass Memories

In windows bright, the colors play,
Reflections of a blessed day.
Each pane a tale, both old and new,
A whisper of the love so true.

The light shines soft on weary souls,
Binding them whole, making them whole.
In every hue, a promise lies,
A glimpse of grace that never dies.

Through time's embrace, we walk the path,
With faith our shield, we find the wrath.
Yet in each shard, a glimpse of peace,
A solace found that will not cease.

With every prayer, the colors glow,
A tapestry of hope we sew.
In stained glass dreams, we are reborn,
In love's warm light, we greet the morn.

So let us gaze with grateful hearts,
In sacred art, where heaven starts.
For in these memories, pure and bright,
We celebrate the endless light.

Evensong for the Brokenhearted

As twilight falls, the shadows creep,
In silence deep, where sorrows sleep.
A hymn of loss, the nightingale sings,
Echoing softly through broken wings.

The stars bear witness to tears shed,
In whispered prayers, we mourn the dead.
Each note of pain, a gentle plea,
For those we love but cannot see.

In moonlit grace, our hearts will mend,
With every heartbeat, love transcends.
A lullaby for souls entwined,
In the rich soil of love combined.

So gather round in the hours late,
Embrace the ache, do not hesitate.
For in this song, we find our way,
A balm for wounds at end of day.

The night will pass, the dawn will break,
We rise anew for love's sweet sake.
Together still, our spirits soar,
In evensong, forevermore.

Holy Dust Upon the Ground

In every grain, a sacred touch,
The earth beneath, we honor much.
With humble hearts, we plant our dreams,
And nurture faith in whispered themes.

The wind carries prayers softly said,
To where the broken find their bed.
In holy dust, the blessings flow,
Roots entwined, our spirits grow.

From ancient hills to valleys wide,
We walk as one, with love our guide.
With open arms, we share the load,
In holy dust, we find the road.

Each step we take, a story told,
Of lives redeemed and hearts made bold.
In sacred soil, our hopes take flight,
As dawn erupts from depths of night.

So here we stand, in trust we dwell,
In holy dust, all is made well.
For every grain, a promise found,
In love's embrace, we stand our ground.

Love's Prayer in Shadows Cast

In twilight's grip, where shadows lay,
We speak our hearts, in soft array.
A prayer of love in dim-lit hue,
Beneath the stars, renewed and true.

With whispered words, the night draws near,
We crown our hopes with every tear.
In shadows deep, our spirits rise,
A compass set toward endless skies.

Through trials faced and burdens borne,
Our faith ignites like early morn.
In every sigh, a vow persists,
Love's gentle call, our hearts insist.

As night unveils the thin veil bright,
We find our way with steadfast light.
In shadows cast, where dreams have flown,
A tapestry of love we've sewn.

So let us hold in tender grace,
The light that shines upon each face.
In love's embrace, we find our rest,
A prayer entwined, eternally blessed.

A Soul's Descent into Yearning

In silence deep, the spirit calls,
A whisper soft, where shadows fall.
Lost in the echoes of the night,
Hope flickers dim, yet seeks the light.

With every tear, a prayer unfolds,
In sacred dreams, the heart retolds.
A journey through the restless sea,
For love's embrace, my soul's decree.

Each step a weight, each breath a plea,
To find the depth of want and need.
In solitude, the heart must fight,
To conquer dark and claim the light.

Yet in this vale of endless prayer,
The yearning grows with every care.
A dance of fate, entwined and true,
The soul ascends, the spirit grew.

I stand before the holy gaze,
In trials born of earthly maze.
With every flame, the heart does soar,
A soul's descent to yearning's door.

Sacred Echoes of Lost Embrace

Within the halls where shadows dwell,
Resounds a hymn, a tale to tell.
Two hearts entwined, yet worlds apart,
An echo lingers in the heart.

The moments shared, now veiled in time,
A silent prayer, a distant chime.
In sacred realms where spirits soar,
The lost embrace begs to restore.

In every touch, a fleeting grace,
A dance remembered, love's sweet trace.
Yet fate conspired, a cruel decree,
To part the bond, set longing free.

Now in the night, I search the skies,
Where stars bear witness, ancient sighs.
For though we walk on separate ways,
The echoes linger, love's soft praise.

A whisper calls through sacred air,
Of what was lost, and all we share.
In every prayer, I seek your face,
In sacred echoes, lost embrace.

The Martyrdom of Desire

In shadows deep, the heart does bleed,
A martyr's tale, a silent creed.
For every wish unvoiced, a cost,
In longing's grip, the soul is lost.

Desire burns with a holy fire,
Yet it brings forth a deep desire.
In whispered nights, my heart shall plead,
For love untouched, an endless need.

Each prayer a dagger, sharp and bright,
In fervent quest beneath the night.
The path of want, a winding road,
The weight of hope, a heavy load.

With every sigh, a life laid bare,
In yearning's name, the soul's despair.
Yet in the struggle, beauty's found,
In martyrdom, love's sacred ground.

Eclipsed in shadows, a dream will rise,
Through all the tears, a love defies.
For while I suffer, still I aspire,
To find redemption in this fire.

The Unspoken Testament of Two

In silent glances, truths collide,
A love concealed, yet none can hide.
An unspoken bond, a tender vow,
Between our souls, the moment's now.

With every heartbeat, whispers weave,
In secret places, hearts believe.
A testament in soft refrain,
In shadows cast, we feel the strain.

Amidst the noise of life's cruel jest,
We carve a path, our hearts confessed.
For in this world of fleeting time,
Our souls converge, a sacred rhyme.

Yet words are lost in tangled fear,
The silent ache that draws you near.
With every breath, a prayer we send,
A silent hope for hearts to mend.

So let our souls take flight anew,
In every glance, in all we do.
The unspoken tale forever spins,
For love, undying, never ends.

Celestial Tears on a Silent Night

In stillness where the shadows sleep,
Stars weep softly from the deep.
Each droplet glimmers with lost grace,
A whisper shared in this holy space.

Moonlight dances on the frost,
Reminding us of what was lost.
The night's embrace, so cold, so light,
Guides our souls through endless night.

Unseen hands hold close our fears,
As past and present intertwine in tears.
For every sigh that meets the breeze,
Hope lingers on the whispering trees.

We gather here, hearts intertwined,
With every prayer, the sacred signed.
Celestial echoes find their way,
In silent nights, where dreams do stay.

Let us rise on these soft wings,
With every note that the night spirit sings.
Together we stand, come what may,
In the celestial tears of this solemn sway.

Pilgrims of the Untouched Realm

We journey forth, with spirits high,
Through fields of faith beneath the sky.
Each step we take, a sacred vow,
To seek the truth in the here and now.

With hearts aflame, we traverse the lands,
In quiet prayers, our fate still stands.
Untouched by doubt, we wander free,
The whispers guide our destiny.

Mountains rise like ancient wise,
Holding secrets of the skies.
Through valleys deep, we find our call,
In unity, we shall not fall.

Every brook that sings our song,
Reminds us where our hearts belong.
In every shadow, light does gleam,
As pilgrims chase the sacred dream.

Together, hand in hand, we walk,
Through paths untraveled, we humbly talk.
With every step, our spirits soar,
In the untouched realm, forevermore.

The Covenant of Broken Dreams

In shadows cast by fading light,
We gather close to share our plight.
Dreams once bright, now scattered dust,
We bind them here with faith and trust.

Each whispered hope, a prayer laid bare,
A vow to mend what life may tear.
In brokenness, our hearts align,
Through struggle blooms the sacred vine.

Fingers entwined, our stories weave,
In every thread, a chance to grieve.
Yet in the ache, a gift is found,
In sacred ground, our love profound.

For every dream that slipped away,
In sorrow's arms, new visions stay.
A covenant forged in trials faced,
Hope's gentle song cannot be erased.

Let tears be rivers that cleanse our soul,
As we gather strength and become whole.
In the fractured light, we find our gleam,
Together we rise from broken dreams.

Hymns of the Heart's Solitude

In silence deep, the spirit sings,
Hymns of heart that solitude brings.
Among the stars, the whispers call,
A sacred echo, a lover's thrall.

Each note a prayer, softly spoken,
A bond of love, unbroken.
With every breath, the heavens sigh,
In solitude, we learn to fly.

Embrace the night, let worries cease,
Find solace in the heart's release.
For in the quiet, light is known,
A garden where the soul has grown.

Through woven threads of time and space,
We carve our path, our sacred place.
In hymn and heart, we find our song,
In solitude, together we belong.

May every tear fall like soft rain,
Washing clean the scars of pain.
In the hush, our spirits meet,
In hymns of solitude, we are complete.

Divine Compass in a Labyrinth of Desire

In shadows deep where whispers dwell,
The heart seeks light, a sacred bell.
Each turn reveals a fleeting grace,
A glimpse of hope, a warm embrace.

Temptations call, their echoes loud,
But faith stands firm, unbowed, unbowed.
Through tangled paths, the spirit roams,
Guided by love, it finds its homes.

The night may fall with heavy sighs,
Yet dawn will paint the waiting skies.
In every choice, a lesson learned,
In every step, a dream returned.

Let not despair steal joy away,
For grace will greet the breaking day.
With every doubt, the soul ascends,
A labyrinth where love transcends.

With every breath, a prayer we weave,
In gratitude, our hearts believe.
For in this maze, divinely spun,
The compass points to love begun.

Manuscript of a Fractured Promise

In parchment worn, the words betray,
A sovereign vow that slipped away.
Each line a tear, a story torn,
A melody of hope, forlorn.

What sacred vows did we neglect?
In silence deep, did we reject?
The ink now fades, a ghostly hue,
Yet love remains, in shreds anew.

Footprints linger on time's soft sand,
A map of dreams we once had planned.
In shadows cast, our truths reside,
In whispered thoughts, the heart confides.

But broken vows can still inspire,
A phoenix from the flames of fire.
Each scar a tale, a gift bestowed,
In faith, the heart's resilience growed.

In every loss, a sacred sign,
A path unseen through love divine.
So let us write with courage true,
A manuscript of me and you.

The Epistle of Unreturned Affection

In silence thick, a heart does pen,
Words that echo, longing when.
A parchment holds the tears unshed,
Love's quiet plea, a hope misread.

Each letter inked with dreams untold,
In shadows cast, a heart grown bold.
Yet every line, a bitter taste,
Affection's call, so cruelly chaste.

The stars above know every sigh,
Each wish that trembles, hopes that fly.
Though silence reigns where love should sing,
In solitude, the heart takes wing.

For unreturned, yet still it glows,
A luminous spark that gently flows.
In quietude, the spirit beams,
A flame of love that always dreams.

So pen my heart in twilight's glow,
An epistle sent, though you won't know.
In gentle whispers, truth shall swell,
In every word, my soul's farewell.

Crossroads of the Heart's Solitude

At the crossroads where silence dwells,
The heart in waiting softly swells.
A choice to make, a path to tread,
Each turn a question left unsaid.

Here echoes linger of dreams once sought,
In shadows cast, the battles fought.
A sacred space where hope abides,
In solitude, the spirit guides.

What lights the way when night is near?
A flicker of faith, a glimpse sincere.
In every decision, a journey new,
A crossroads met where love breaks through.

Yet still the ache of parts unknown,
A heart as vast as fields unshown.
In every pause, a chance to see,
The beauty in the let it be.

So here I stand, in peace, though torn,
A place where souls might be reborn.
At life's crossroads, I shall embrace,
The quiet strength of love's true grace.

The Silent Sacrifice of Devotion

In quiet shadows, hearts abide,
With whispered prayers, the soul confides.
Through trials faced and tears that fall,
A silent strength, the faithful call.

In dawn's embrace, devotion sways,
Beneath the weight of countless days.
Each sacrifice, a fragrant bloom,
In sacred light, dispelling gloom.

The humble path, a winding way,
Where love, like stars, will guide and stay.
In every moment, faith persists,
In quietude, grace softly twists.

When doubts arise, when shadows loom,
The heart ignites, dispelling gloom.
With every beat, a hymn unfolds,
In silent oaths, true love upholds.

And so we walk this hallowed ground,
In fervent peace, our souls are found.
The silent sacrifice, a sacred thread,
In every heart, devotion spread.

Spiritual Yearnings

In the stillness of the night,
Whispers call to hearts in flight.
Yearnings rise like fragrant smoke,
In every spirit, a longing spoke.

Beyond the veil of earthly ties,
The soul ascends to boundless skies.
In silent prayers, we seek the light,
Guiding us through the darkest night.

With open hands and weary hearts,
We gather hopes while grace imparts.
In every twist and turn of fate,
Our spirits lift, we contemplate.

The echoes of the ages call,
In ancient hymns that rise and fall.
For in our yearnings, we find the way,
To realms unseen, where spirits play.

As rivers flow to meet the sea,
Our hopes converge, eternally.
In every yearning, love does dwell,
A sacred truth we know so well.

Flesh and Bone

In this vessel of flesh and bone,
A spirit dances, not alone.
Each heartbeat whispers life's sweet song,
In the ebb and flow, we all belong.

With scars of joy and pain adorned,
A testament of love, reborn.
In fragile forms, we find our grace,
Embracing all, our sacred space.

In shadows cast by time's embrace,
We lift our eyes to seek a trace.
Of something greater, vast, divine,
In every glance, His love does shine.

Bound by the earth, yet spirit soars,
Through trials faced, our faith restores.
In every breath, a prayer we weave,
In bone and flesh, we dare believe.

Through life's tempest, we stand as one,
In unity, our hearts have won.
For flesh and bone, though weak they seem,
Hold sacred truths within the dream.

Sacred Threads of Care

In woven lives, our hearts entwine,
With threads of care, a love divine.
Through trials shared and laughter sweet,
In every moment, love's heartbeat.

The fabric strong, yet gently worn,
In kindness given, souls are borne.
Each shared glance, a silent vow,
In sacred trust, the here and now.

With helping hands and open hearts,
We gather strength as love imparts.
In acts of grace, our spirits rise,
Beneath the watchful, loving skies.

Through woven paths of joy and strife,
We nurture dreams, we breathe new life.
In every stitch, a prayer shall flow,
In sacred threads, we come to know.

For in each bond, a sacred sign,
Of love that flows, a grand design.
In threads of care, our spirits blend,
In every heart, a love to send.

The Altar to Unfulfilled Dreams

Atop the altar, dreams reside,
In whispered prayers, hopes coincide.
With trembling hands, we lay them down,
In faith we stand, our dreams renown.

Each unfulfilled, a lesson learned,
In quiet moments, our hearts have turned.
Through trials faced, the soul ascends,
In yearning still, the spirit mends.

For every wish that fades away,
A brighter path begins to play.
In every glimpse of what could be,
We find the light that sets us free.

Each tear that falls, a seed is sown,
In barren lands, new dreams are grown.
With every breath, a hope reborn,
In darkness deep, a light is worn.

So on this altar of regret,
We gather strength, we won't forget.
For dreams may wane, but hope remains,
In every heart, love's promise reigns.

The Oracle of Yearning Souls

In shadows deep, the whispers call,
Beneath the weight of fate's cruel thrall.
Hearts aflame, a longing burn,
To endless skies, their hopes return.

With mournful song, the spirits cry,
For love that left and dreams gone dry.
Yet in this void, the light persists,
A promise held in tender mist.

Each prayer ascends like fragrant smoke,
A testament to words unspoke.
In every soul, a quest divine,
To bridge the gap and intertwine.

The oracle speaks of paths unseen,
Of galaxies where love has been.
In every tear, a story told,
Of yearning hearts and shadows bold.

Though trials come and doubts may rise,
In faith we find our sweetest ties.
For every soul is bound by grace,
In every void, a hidden place.

Lamentations Beneath the Starlit Veil

Beneath the stars, the mourners weep,
In silence deep, their secrets keep.
The nightingale sings of lost delight,
As shadows dance in the pale moonlight.

Each tear that falls like silent rain,
Echoes of love, the bitter pain.
The heavens sigh, a gentle breath,
Acknowledging the weight of death.

In every heart, a story waits,
Of common joys and twisted fates.
The stars above, they seem so near,
Yet in the night, we drown in fear.

With wisdom gleaned from sacred lore,
We seek the path that offers more.
Transcend the loss, embrace the night,
In darkness, find the hidden light.

Amongst the shadows, spirits roam,
In search of peace, they find a home.
Beneath the veil, their voices blend,
In unity, they transcend.

Sacred Grail of Unrequited Affection

In quiet halls where echoes dwell,
A heart entwined in wishing well.
The sacred grail, a longing cup,
To sip the joy, yet never sup.

Each glance a spark, a fleeting flame,
The dance of hope is never tame.
For love unshared, a whispered song,
In every note, the ghosts belong.

With prayers adorned in silken threads,
We weave the dreams we dare not shed.
In every heartbeat, tales of woe,
Unrequited, yet still they grow.

The path is steep, yet unafraid,
We chase the shadows love has laid.
With every sigh, we claim our right,
To hold the dawn against the night.

In crystal chalice, hope bestows,
The strength to bear what love bestows.
Though yearning stays and hearts may ache,
The sacred grail, no true heart breaks.

The Path of Wandering Hearts

In gentle winds, the wanderers tread,
With open hearts, where dreams are led.
Each step a prayer upon the ground,
A symphony of souls unbound.

The stars above, a guiding light,
Illuminate the paths of night.
In every turn, a choice to make,
With courage found in love's true wake.

Through valleys deep and mountains high,
The weary hearts lift up their sigh.
For in the pain, a lesson stands,
In every fall, the heart expands.

United by a sacred thread,
An odyssey where angels tread.
With each heartbeat, echoes prove,
The path of wandering leads to love.

With spirits bold and dreams alive,
In every soul, the flames survive.
Together forged, we seek the flame,
On paths where every heart can claim.

The Pilgrimage of Longing

Through valleys deep, my spirit roams,
In search of grace, I call it home.
The whispers soft, like echoes near,
Guide my heart, dissolve my fear.

Each step I take upon this ground,
In every tear, the lost are found.
For what is life but sacred quest,
In faith I stand, my soul at rest.

Beneath the stars, the journey calls,
Through shadows dense, the promise falls.
A beacon bright, in night's embrace,
Leading me forth to endless grace.

With every dawn, a hope reborn,
Through trials hard, I'm ever torn.
Yet in this strife, the spirit sings,
For peace awaits on healing wings.

So let my heart, with fervor beat,
In every prayer, I find retreat.
The pilgrimage, a path divine,
In longing's depth, my soul will shine.

Chasing Incense in the Dark

In shadows thick, the fragrance glows,
A whisper sweet, where silence flows.
With searching heart and open mind,
I chase the trails the holy find.

The night is filled with sacred breath,
In murmurs soft, we dance with death.
A cloud of smoke, the spirit's grace,
Draws me near to the sacred place.

Each tender puff, a prayer that soars,
As I align with ancient doors.
In darkened realms, the light ignites,
To guide the lost on starry nights.

Oh, let the incense lift my soul,
To join the chorus, pure and whole.
In every waft, I find the spark,
Of love that shines within the dark.

So here I stand, with heart so bare,
In every breath, a sacred prayer.
Through darkened paths, my spirit soars,
To chase the light forevermore.

Vows Amidst the Celestial Silence

In silence deep, where spirits dwell,
I speak my vows, the heart's soft swell.
In cosmic night, my promise rings,
As stars descend on silken wings.

Each whispered word, a thread divine,
Entwines with fate, my soul's design.
In every breath, a pact is sealed,
In quietude, my heart revealed.

The heavens watch, with tender care,
In sacred trust, our souls laid bare.
Together bound, through trials past,
In love's embrace, we hold steadfast.

As galaxies swirl in cosmic grace,
I pledge my heart, my sacred space.
In this vast realm, our spirits blend,
With every vow, the stars ascend.

So listen close, in stillness found,
To hear the love, profound, unbound.
In celestial silence, hearts ignite,
Forever joined, in endless light.

Heartstrings Pulled by Angels

When shadows creep and doubts arise,
I feel the pull of unseen ties.
With gentle hands, the angels lead,
My heart awakes, my soul's freed.

Their whispers soft as morning dew,
Remind me of the love that's true.
With every tug, the strings align,
In harmony, our hearts entwine.

Through trials faced, and paths unknown,
The angels guide me towards the throne.
Each breath a note, a sacred song,
In this grand symphony, we belong.

In every tear, a lesson learned,
In every turn, my heart has yearned.
Yet with their grace, I'm gently steered,
By light divine, I'm ever cheered.

So let the music swell and rise,
A testament beneath the skies.
For in this dance, my soul takes flight,
Heartstrings pulled by angels' light.

My Heart, a Broken Vessel

My heart lies shattered, a fragile shard,
In the stillness, I search for grace.
Each crack a story, a journey marred,
Yet hope's soft whisper fills this space.

Within the chaos, a sacred light,
Illuminates shadows of my despair.
In brokenness, I find the fight,
To mend the vessel, a healing prayer.

The pieces linger, a tapestry worn,
Woven with love that can never fade.
In storms of sorrow, I won't be torn,
For in my heart, His truth is laid.

With every heartbeat, I hear the call,
To rise anew from the ashes thrown.
In my surrender, I shall not fall,
For my spirit's strength is now my own.

Though vessel broken, it holds a song,
A melody born of purest light.
In each fracture, I find I belong,
To the divine, forever bright.

The Cherubic Tear

From heaven's gate, a cherub weeps,
A tear like starlight graces the land.
In silent prayers, the sorrow creeps,
Imbued with love, a gentle hand.

Each droplet weaves a tale of grace,
Of burdens borne and hearts laid bare.
In sacred space, we find our place,
To catch the tear, to learn, to share.

Beneath the weight of the world we sigh,
Yet in the tear, there lies a spark.
A promise holds as we lift our eye,
To seek the light within the dark.

A cherub's tear, a soft embrace,
Reminds us of the love we bear.
In each sadness, we find a trace,
Of divine presence everywhere.

So let us cherish the tear so pure,
For in our sorrow, we shall find,
The strength to heal, the heart to endure,
With every drop, our souls entwined.

Faith in Half-Remembered Touches

In twilight whispers, echoes call,
Of half-remembered yet sacred ties.
With faith we rise, despite the fall,
Through whispered dreams, our spirit flies.

Each touch a thread, spun from the past,
Woven in shadows of fleeting grace.
Though moments fade, the love holds fast,
In every heartbeat, you find your place.

Through veils of doubt, your essence stays,
Like sunlight filtering through the trees.
In half-remembered, love's gentle rays,
Illuminate paths, like a gentle breeze.

In every heartbeat, faith persists,
A solace sought in forgotten days.
In quiet moments, the spirit insists,
That love transcends all memory's haze.

So let us hold these touches dear,
In each embrace, let our hearts expand.
For faith, though blurred, shall always steer,
Our souls together, forever hand in hand.

A Litany for Relics of Love

In sacred halls, the echoes ring,
For relics cherished, we humbly sing.
Each memory preserved, a vibrant thread,
In the tapestry of love, we are wed.

We call upon the days of old,
Where laughter bloomed, and hearts were bold.
The relics speak of joy and pain,
A journey shared through sun and rain.

With every token, we raise a prayer,
For love once lived beyond compare.
The whispers linger in the air,
With gratitude, we lay them bare.

For in the fragments, the truth is found,
That love's sweet essence shall abound.
Let not forget what bonds unite,
In every relic shines the light.

So gather round this sacred space,
To honor love, to seek its grace.
In litany, we find our way,
Through relics of love, we shall stay.

A Canticle for the Forgotten

In shadowed halls where silence clings,
Voices lost in time still sing.
Whispers of hope, of grace bestowed,
Their light is dimmed, yet still they glowed.

Beneath the weight of sorrow's veil,
Faith persists through every tale.
The broken hearts, they find their place,
As love transcends in whispered grace.

Each step we take upon this ground,
Remembers those who once were found.
With every prayer, we set them free,
In sacred bond, we too shall be.

With open arms, the heavens weep,
For every soul that yearns to leap.
In unity, the past we hold,
Together, we shall break the mold.

So let us sing for those in plight,
Their spirits guide us through the night.
For in the dark, a spark resides,
A canticle through love abides.

Serenity Amidst the Temptation

In gardens lush, the serpent coils,
Temptation thrives where innocence toils.
Yet still, a voice, soft as the breeze,
Calls us to gaze beyond the trees.

With every fruit that catches eye,
We ponder worth as whispers fly.
But deep within, a truth unfolds,
A peace that shuns what lust beholds.

In quietude, the heart takes rest,
Resisting calls that leave unrest.
Through stillness, find the sacred way,
A seraph's path to grace display.

When chaos stirs and doubts arise,
The soul ascends, the spirit flies.
For strength renewed through faith we claim,
In serenity, we know His name.

So let the winds of trial blow,
With steadfast hearts, our spirit grow.
In every choice, let love preside,
Amidst temptation, He'll be our guide.

The Serpent's Whisper of Desire

In twilight's hush, the serpent speaks,
A subtle charm that tempts the weak.
Desire's voice, both sweet and sly,
Draws us near with a velvet lie.

With every word, a promise made,
To fill the void, our souls betrayed.
Yet in this dance of dark design,
A spark remains, a love divine.

We walk the line of right and wrong,
As echoes of the past grow strong.
But in our hearts, a truth ignites,
To guard our souls through darkest nights.

When shadows cast their haunting spell,
And silence births a hidden hell,
We'll raise our gaze to skies of gold,
A strength reborn, our faith our hold.

For though temptation lures us near,
The love, true love, is crystal clear.
In every heart, a flame shall blaze,
Defying all the serpent's ways.

A Resurrection of Past Hearts

From ashes deep, where memories sleep,
A light is cast, our souls shall leap.
The past entangles, yet hope remains,
In every tear, a lesson gains.

Through trials faced, we learn to rise,
Like phoenix wings against the skies.
Forgiveness weaves the fabric tight,
A tapestry of love and light.

Each heart that yearned in silence deep,
Awakens now from distant sleep.
With every smile, a story told,
In unity, our dreams enfold.

So let us gather, hand in hand,
For past and present, we shall stand.
In sacred moments, we find our part,
A resurrection of past hearts.

In harmony, the spirits soar,
For love unites, forevermore.
As we embrace the paths we walked,
The whispers of the past, now talked.

A Covenant with the Stars

In the night, the heavens breathe,
Whispers of ancient truth we weave.
Galaxies dance in sacred grace,
Guiding lost souls through time and space.

Promises written in shimmering light,
Each twinkle a beacon, a loving sight.
Stars offer hope, their glow divine,
In their embrace, our spirits align.

The cosmos speaks in silent songs,
Uniting hearts where each belongs.
A pact unbroken, a flame of trust,
In starlit realms, we rise from dust.

Celestial bodies, our brothers, our kin,
In their watchful gaze, we begin again.
With every dawn, our faith shall rise,
As we seek the grace in endless skies.

So let us journey, hand in hand,
With the stars above, a timeless band.
In faith's embrace, we'll find our way,
A covenant of love that will never sway.

Darkness Beneath the Holy Light

In shadows deep where silence roams,
The heartache lingers, far from homes.
Yet, holy light breaks through the night,
Illuminating paths with hope so bright.

In every soul, the struggle burns,
Seeking peace as the world turns.
A flicker of faith through veils of fear,
Invites the weary to draw near.

Beneath the grace, the darkness sways,
Yet love's embrace forever stays.
In troubled hearts, a promise blooms,
For even in night, He clears our glooms.

With every tear that gently falls,
The sacred whispers, salvation calls.
In darkness deep, we find the spark,
An everlasting light within the dark.

So lift your gaze to love's embrace,
In trials faced, we find our place.
Through sacred bonds, we rise anew,
With holy light, we journey through.

Echoes of Forgotten Promises

In the stillness where silence dwells,
Echoes whisper of forgotten spells.
Promises made on a fragrant breeze,
Carried softly through ancient trees.

The heart recalls the vows once sworn,
In twilight's grace, the spirit's worn.
What was lost still calls our name,
In shadows deep, no need for shame.

Through time's embrace, we learn to see,
Each scar a lesson, a part of me.
In every path that we have tread,
Lies divine truth, where hope is spread.

Though whispers fade in the passing years,
The sacred binds remain, not fears.
In every pulse, the promise stays,
An echo of love through all our days.

So let us honor what was once claimed,
With open hearts, our souls inflamed.
In the light of spirit, we'll find our way,
As echoes of love guide us each day.

The Fading Halo of Affection

In twilight hours, the halo dims,
Love's warm glow fades from the hymns.
Yet, in the silence, whispers bloom,
A lingering fragrance fills the room.

The heart remembers tender grace,
In fleeting moments, a sacred space.
Though times may change, love's bond is true,
In each heartbeat, I still find you.

With every sunset, a prayer is spun,
For all that's lost, for all that's won.
In fading light, the spirit soars,
And love remains, forever endures.

Through trials faced and journeys long,
The soul will sing its timeless song.
A halo fading, yet ever near,
In shadows bright, I hold you dear.

So take my hand, we'll walk the line,
In every heartbeat, your heart is mine.
Fading halo, our truth remains,
In love's embrace, through joy and pains.

Devotion in the Shadow of Absence

In the stillness, I seek Your grace,
Every prayer a whispered trace.
Though silence wraps my weary soul,
Your light, my heart, it does console.

Through the void, a flicker stays,
Guiding me through shadowed ways.
In absence deep, my spirit knows,
Your presence felt in gentle throes.

Morning sun, a herald bright,
Calls me forth to trust in light.
With every step, I feel the link,
Between my heart and love's great ink.

Though distance stretches far and wide,
In faith's embrace, I will abide.
Your love, a beacon, ever near,
In shadow's depth, I shed my fear.

In devotion's name, I stand strong,
With every note, a sacred song.
Though absence looms, my heart will sing,
In faith's embrace, new hope takes wing.

Songs of a Faithful Heart's Despair

In the night, my heart does ache,
Each wish a tremor, dreams that break.
Yet in the dark, a candle glows,
A prayer, a song, my spirit knows.

For every tear that falls like rain,
I offer up a sacred pain.
In shadows cast by fleeting light,
I seek the dawn, a hopeful sight.

Though faith is tried by trials near,
I cling to whispers, soft and clear.
Each note a promise, sweet and raw,
My heart an altar, life's great law.

Despair may wrap its chains around,
Yet in the depths, Your love is found.
From sorrow's depth, a song will rise,
A faithful heart cannot disguise.

Let every beat in rhythm flow,
With trust that in the dark, You know.
Through every doubt, I'll find my way,
For in despair, I learn to pray.

The Altar of Forgotten Promises

Upon this stone, the silence waits,
Echoes of love, and heavy fates.
Forgotten vows, they whisper low,
In shadows deep, where lost hopes grow.

With trembling hands, I lift my voice,
In sacred space, I make my choice.
To seek the light where none may tread,
To honor dreams by grace once led.

Though promises may lie in dust,
My faith persists in sacred trust.
With every breath, I find anew,
The path of grace, a light so true.

The altar stands with scars of time,
Where once was joy, and now, a rhyme.
Yet in this space, I find retreat,
To sow the seeds of love complete.

Forgiveness blooms where hope is sown,
A testament to love we've grown.
In every stone, a story weaves,
The altar waits, as time believes.

Prayers Amidst the Ruins of Desire

In ruins of dreams, a heart did break,
Yet in the silence, new paths I take.
With every prayer, a seed is sown,
In barren lands, my spirit's grown.

Amidst the ashes, faith ignites,
Like distant stars on darkest nights.
Each yearning thought, each whispered plea,
A bridge to what's yet meant to be.

Though passion fades, my heart will burn,
In longing's grip, I patiently learn.
The remnants speak of love's sweet call,
As embers glow from shadows' fall.

Each prayer a thread, weaving the past,
Binding my heart to joys that last.
In ruins deep, I find the light,
That turns my sorrow into flight.

So let my spirit dance anew,
In every prayer, a promise true.
Amidst the ruins, hope's flame will rise,
From ashes deep, my heart defies.

Miracles Lost in Time

In shadows cast by silent nights,
Where hope once danced in humble lights,
The whispers of the past now fade,
Yet miracles in silence played.

Each moment lost, a treasured thread,
In time's embrace, where dreams are wed,
On wings of faith, we seek the dawn,
To find the light where love has drawn.

Through trials deep, we seek the spark,
In faithful hearts, we leave a mark,
For every tear, a lesson sown,
In miracles, we're never alone.

Yet memories, like echoes, call,
In fading light, we rise or fall,
From ashes, hope begins to rise,
As miracles weave through our sighs.

So take my hand, let us ascend,
Through time and faith, we'll learn to mend,
With every star, a prayer we weave,
In every heart, true love believes.

The Atonement of a Shattered Bond

A fractured love, in silence wept,
Promises made, and secrets kept,
In weary hearts, the shadows dwell,
Yet hope remains, a whispered spell.

Through trials faced, we seek our way,
In brokenness, our souls still pray,
For bonds that bind can mend in grace,
In love's embrace, we find our place.

Forgiveness flows like gentle streams,
In open hearts, we chase our dreams,
With every tear, a path we tread,
To find the light where once we bled.

Through darkest nights, we'll seek the flame,
In unity, we'll rise again,
Each step we take, a promise new,
With faith restored, our love shines through.

Let time be kind, let hearts be true,
In atonement, our spirits grew,
For shattered bonds can reshape fate,
In love's embrace, we find our state.

Incense of Memories Adrift

In fragrant smoke, the past unfolds,
Stories whispered, secrets told,
Each memory a sacred note,
In incense dreams, our souls emote.

The flickering flame, a guide so bright,
Through shadowed paths, we seek the light,
For every scent, a moment's grace,
In echoes lost, we find our place.

With every breath, a prayer ascends,
To realms above, where love transcends,
In moments pure, our spirits soar,
In incense dreams, we crave for more.

Through trials faced, we learn to rise,
With hearts of courage, we touch the skies,
Each whispered prayer, a fragrant bond,
In memories, our hopes respond.

So let the incense guide our way,
In sacred moments, let us stay,
For in the past, our hearts still drift,
In love embraced, our spirits lift.

Revelations from the Echoing Void

In silence deep, the void reveals,
The truths concealed, the pain that heals,
Each echo lost, a whispered call,
In shadows tall, we rise or fall.

Through darkened paths, the light will shine,
In every heart, a sacred sign,
For in the depths, the spirit roams,
In quiet grace, the soul finds homes.

With every breath, revelations flow,
Through trials faced, we learn and grow,
In emptiness, the heart takes flight,
In echoes felt, we seek the light.

As galaxies spin in endless grace,
We find our path, we seek our place,
For in the void, the truth is born,
In every loss, a heart reborn.

So hear the echoes, soft and clear,
In sacred spaces, draw them near,
For every void, a chance to see,
In revelations, we find our plea.

Whispers Beneath the Altar

In silence low, the candles flicker,
Soft prayers rise, the heart grows thicker.
Beneath the stone, a sacred breath,
Resides the hope, defying death.

In shadows deep, the spirits call,
With every tear, we rise, we fall.
The altar bears, our burdened sighs,
In faith's embrace, the soul flies high.

Through whispers soft, the echo flows,
In humble praise, the spirit grows.
Together bound, in love we stand,
In grace, we find, a guiding hand.

As twilight dims, the world takes pause,
In every beat, we share a cause.
Beneath the altar, hearts entwine,
In sacred love, our dreams align.

Sacred Shadows of the Heart

In quiet night, the shadows dance,
Each flickering star, a whispered chance.
The heart seeks light, in darkness deep,
In silence found, our secrets keep.

With every breath, a prayer ascends,
In sacred realms, where spirit bends.
The shadow speaks, in tender hue,
With every glance, the soul renews.

In sacred vows, our spirits soar,
Through trials fought, we love them more.
In every shadow, hope resides,
With open hearts, the truth abides.

Through sacred bonds, we find our way,
In every dawn, the light will stay.
Embrace the night, for love will spark,
In sacred shadows, we leave our mark.

Divine Embrace

In gentle folds of silken grace,
We find our home, a warm embrace.
With lifted hands, our spirits entwined,
In harmony sweet, our hearts aligned.

The heavens sigh, a tender balm,
In every storm, there lies a calm.
Through trials faced, in love we stand,
In divine touch, we hold each hand.

With every breath, the hymn resounds,
In sacred joy, our truth abounds.
Together strong, we rise anew,
In every moment, our faith rings true.

In whispered dreams, the night unfolds,
In loving arms, our story's told.
Through light and dark, we journey far,
In divine embrace, we shine like stars.

Forgotten Touch

In whispers lost, where shadows dwell,
A silent prayer, a hidden spell.
With every glance, a memory prays,
In tender grace, our heart displays.

Though time may fade, the truth remains,
In every tear, in every gain.
With longing hearts, we seek the light,
In memories held, we find our plight.

In gentle folds of love's embrace,
The forgotten touch, we still can trace.
Through shadows cast, we hold the past,
In warmth of hope, our love will last.

In silent rooms, where echoes play,
A soft reminder of love's sway.
In every heartbeat, a distant call,
In forgotten touch, we rise, we fall.

Prayers on the Edge of Night

In twilight's hush, our voices blend,
With every prayer, the night's a friend.
Beneath the stars, we seek the calm,
In whispered hopes, we find our psalm.

The moonlight glows, a guiding light,
In every heart, a spark ignites.
With open arms, we share our fears,
In sacred silence, we dry our tears.

Through paths unknown, we walk with grace,
In every step, love finds its place.
As day surrenders, we rise in flight,
With prayers unfurled, on edge of night.

In dreams we soar, our spirits free,
Together bound, in unity.
As stars align, our hopes ignite,
In prayers aloft, we chase the light.

The Rite of Beloved Absences

In the silence where echoes dwell,
Whispers of love weave a sacred spell.
Memories linger, soft as a prayer,
Yearning for moments that once filled the air.

Stars align in the velvet night,
Guiding lost souls in their quest for light.
Each tear a testament, each sigh a song,
In absence we learn where we truly belong.

The heart, a vessel of faith and pain,
Holds the fragments, like drops of rain.
From shadows emerges a flicker of hope,
In the distance, we find ways to cope.

Together we're scattered, but never apart,
Decked in virtues that shape the heart.
In the garden of longing where dreams take flight,
We find solace in the endless night.

So we gather these moments, sacred and dear,
In the rite of absence, love conquers fear.
With every farewell, a promise remains,
To cherish the bond that forever sustains.

Benedictions on Broken Wings

High above where the angels sing,
Love's benediction serenely takes wing.
With a whisper of grace, the spirit takes flight,
Through valleys of sorrow, to embrace the light.

Each scar a story, each tear a prayer,
In the heart's quiet corners, we lay ourselves bare.
Amidst the journey, we gather the shards,
Transforming the pain into sacred regards.

Through the storms of despair, we rise and we fall,
In brokenness, beauty unites us all.
Every heartbeat a melody, fiercely it sings,
In the tenderest moments, the solace it brings.

Though the path may be shadowed, we've weathered the night,
Cloaked in the promise of morning's sweet light.
With courage, we navigate love's winding way,
In the heart's gentle cradle, forever we stay.

So let the wings flutter, though tattered they be,
For in every surrender, we're truly set free.
A blessing bestowed on the souls that have soared,
Speaks of the love that eternally roared.

The Hidden Sanctum of Heartache

Within the shadows, a sanctuary lies,
Where heartache dwells and hope never dies.
In whispers of solace, we hear the divine,
Each sigh we release turns to radiance shy.

The cracks in our armor, a testament true,
To the strength that resides in me and in you.
Like flowers that bloom in a tempest's embrace,
We gather our courage, we carry our grace.

In the depths of despair, a light starts to gleam,
Illuminating the fragments of a shattered dream.
We kindle the fire that once burned so bright,
With every heartbeat, we reclaim our sight.

Moments of stillness, echoes of pain,
In this hidden refuge, love's lessons remain.
Though heartache may linger like shadows at dusk,
In every heartbeat, there lies a deep trust.

So we honor the journey, the road has been rough,
In the sanctum we find that our spirits are tough.
In unity, we rise, hand in hand, we shall stand,
Embracing each bruise as part of the grand plan.

Cherished Shadows of a Distant Embrace

In the twilight's glow, we find our refrain,
Cherished shadows dance on the whispering plain.
Embraces remembered, though distance divides,
In the realm of the heart, love never hides.

Each memory cradled, like secrets they keep,
In the still of the night, we treasure and weep.
The echoes of laughter entwine with our tears,
In the tapestry woven with hopes and our fears.

Though time may be fleeting, the essence remains,
In the language of spirit, no barrier chains.
We cherish the moments, no matter how far,
For love knows no limits, it reaches like stars.

Through the whispers of ages, we grow and we learn,
In the lessons of heartache, our passions still burn.
In the shadows of longing, light softly breaks,
In the depth of the silence, a beacon awakes.

So we gather our shadows, let them take flight,
In the essence of love, we are never out of sight.
For even in distance, our souls intertwine,
In cherished embraces, our hearts remain blind.

The Ascension of Longing Souls

Upon the heights where whispers rise,
Longing souls in silent ties.
They reach for light, for grace divine,
In the embrace of love's design.

Through veils of tears, they seek the dawn,
With every breath, in faith, they yawn.
The heavens open, spirits soar,
To find the peace they've sought before.

In unity, their voices blend,
With hopes and dreams, their hearts suspend.
Each step a prayer, each glance a sign,
In sacred quest, their souls align.

The winds of fate, like whispers flow,
Guiding paths where longing grows.
In every heart a spark ignites,
In pursuit of sublime heights.

Together now, the chorus swells,
In harmony, their truth compels.
Through trials faced and sorrows shed,
They rise as one, where angels tread.

The Testament of Tattered Bonds

In shadows deep, where sorrow dwells,
Tattered bonds tell their tales.
Each thread a struggle, worn and frayed,
Yet love remains, though hope betrayed.

Fingers intertwine in prayer's embrace,
Wrapped in memories, time can't erase.
For every tear, a lesson learned,
In heart's forge, their spirit burned.

The weight of myrrh and bitter myrrh,
Fragrance of loss, the heart's soft stir.
Yet, in each crack, the light does seep,
Awakening dreams, from shadows deep.

Through pain endured and storms survived,
The testament speaks, the spirit thrived.
In every parting, souls entwined,
A bond unbroken, love defined.

Raise high the banners of sacred ties,
For in the heart, true love never dies.
With each embrace, let peace accrue,
A testament of hearts so true.

A Sanctuary for Sorrow

In quiet corners, sorrow lays,
A sanctuary where silence stays.
Whispers of grief in sacred space,
Finding solace in love's embrace.

Each tear that falls, a river's grace,
Flowing gently, a healing trace.
They wander through the halls of night,
Searching for a flickering light.

Among the shadows, spirits roam,
With heavy hearts, they seek their home.
In whispered prayers, they're not alone,
For every ache, a strength is grown.

In the stillness, truth prevails,
With every sigh, the spirit sails.
Through pain, the journey finds its way,
To brighter dawns, to hope's new day.

A sanctuary where souls may weep,
Where memories flourish, and love runs deep.
Though sorrow lingers, joy will rise,
In this sacred space, hearts harmonize.

The Divine Dance of Absence

In the stillness, absence plays,
A divine dance in the heart's maze.
Echoes linger where shadows dwell,
In the silence, soft stories swell.

Through empty rooms where laughter fled,
The spirit waltzes, a sacred thread.
With every step, they honor grace,
In the dance of love, they find their place.

In moonlit nights, where memories gleam,
The absence whispers, a timeless dream.
With every beat, a heartbeat's trace,
In the vast void, there lies a space.

Together still, through tears, they glide,
In the dance of absence, side by side.
For every parting, a movement starts,
In the rhythm of longing hearts.

In the embrace of night's soft chance,
They twirl amidst the divine dance.
With every sigh, a story spun,
In the absence, love's never done.

Milton Keynes UK
Ingram Content Group UK Ltd.
UKHW031322271124
451618UK00007B/128